IMAGES
of America

SEGUIN AND
GUADALUPE COUNTY

Otto Baenziger's family, pictured in this 1935 photograph, began a small grocery business in Seguin in 1932. Frugal and hardworking, Baenziger eventually bought the building from W. J. Blumberg that later became the Baenziger Red and White store. Later the Eugene Naumann family and the Henry Upper family also had neighborhood Red and White grocery stores. Baenziger's descendents Harold, Rubin, and their families donated the building in 1991 to become a museum. Thanks to their foresight and generosity and robust community support, the not-for-profit heritage museum has become a part of downtown Seguin in the middle of the historic district and enjoys visitors from Texas, other parts of the United States, and many foreign countries. From left to right are (first row) Melba Baenziger, Nora Baenziger, Otto Baenziger (father), and Herminia Lambrecht Baenziger (wife); (second row) Rubin Baenziger, Ethel "Eddie" Baenziger, Violet Baenziger, and Harold Baenziger. (Courtesy of the Leon Studio Photo Collection of the Seguin-Guadalupe County Heritage Museum.)

ON THE COVER: The intersection of Court Street (U.S. Highway 90) and Austin Street has been the center of downtown Seguin since 1839, when the town was first platted. This photograph from the dawn of the 20th century depicts a Seguin that has not changed much. Many of the original buildings remain, although their edifices and interiors have changed to reflect the times. The roads are now paved, there is a stoplight at the intersection, and the Seguin railway car that operated from the train depot on North Austin Street to downtown is no longer needed. A legend exists that the rail lines remain under the pavement. (Courtesy of the Leon Studio Photo Collection of the Seguin-Guadalupe County Heritage Museum.)

IMAGES
of America

SEGUIN AND
GUADALUPE COUNTY

E. John Gesick Jr. and the
Seguin-Guadalupe County Heritage Museum

ARCADIA
PUBLISHING

Published by Arcadia Publishing
Charleston, South Carolina

Library of Congress Control Number: 2009936035

For all general information contact Arcadia Publishing at:
Telephone 843-853-2070
Fax 843-853-0044
E-mail sales@arcadiapublishing.com
For customer service and orders:
Toll-Free 1-888-313-2665

Visit us on the Internet at www.arcadiapublishing.com

*Dedicated to Willy Weiss and Leon and Nelda Kubala,
founders and owners of the Weiss Studio and
Leon Studio, both community treasures*

CONTENTS

Acknowledgments   6

Introduction   7

1.   Prehistoric and Historic Seguin:
     Environmental and Human Legacies   9

2.   Foundations of Early Seguin:
     Beginnings of a New Era   21

3.   Businesses, Agriculture, and Politics:
     19th and Early 20th Centuries   39

4.   School Days and Churches:
     Then and Now   61

5.   A Crossroads of Commerce:
     1940s–1980s   81

6.   Twenty-first Century Metamorphosis:
     1990s–2010   97

7.   A Legacy from the Past:
     Today and Tomorrow   113

ACKNOWLEDGMENTS

Someone once observed that a single individual seldom ever does compiling and writing, even in the earliest stages. This was certainly true during this pleasant journey into Seguin's past and present.

There are a number of heartfelt thanks to the many who helped in this effort. Pat Kenneaster's cheerful and efficient office management kept the museum on track for its many visitors; Ruth Ann Leal's computer knowledge and patience in the book typing and revisions were more than noteworthy; Beth Lange was stellar and very patient with me on photograph selections and arrangements. Without Stanley Naumann's gifted photographic eye, we would not have the collection that appears in this work. And a big thank-you goes to Michael Murphy and his computer knowledge in working with our layout.

There were many others who shared our journey. Edward Davila, Ramón Salazar Jr., Leonardo Molina, Clarence Little, and Danny Daniels shared their insights of this relatively conservative but forward-thinking community and region that Seguin and Guadalupe County are. Had it not been for Julie Sullivan, Debbie Snyder, and Winter Callaway, the script would have been unintelligible. Thank you so much.

Most importantly, our sincerest thanks go out to the citizens of Seguin-Guadalupe County. After all, if they were not here then this book would not be either.

Unless otherwise noted, all images appear courtesy of the Leon Studio Photo Collection of the Seguin-Guadalupe County Heritage Museum.

INTRODUCTION

Long before the first humans arrived, Seguin and Guadalupe County were underwater. In this region are numerous fossilized artifacts of marine life from millions of years ago. These are evidenced through collections of coral, sharks teeth, algae spore, cephalopods, "devil's toenail" oysters, pelecypops, mastodon teeth, such as "nipple tooth" molars, and skeletal remains, including tusks. Evidence of other animals' activity in this region is the horse, bison, camel, ground sloth, saber tooth tiger, and early armadillos.

With the receding ice age, early human life arrived, leaving behind numerous artifacts of their existence. Soon emerging were extensive trade routes from the coastal regions throughout south-central Texas. These early indigenous peoples were exceptionally advanced in bartering and trading of objects from Arizona, northern Mexico, the lower plains region, and the Southeast.

Numerous encampments dotted the extensive trade routes along the rivers and streams, including the San Marcos River, Guadalupe River, Cibolo Creek, and Geronimo Creek. The largest encampment, just discovered in late 2008, is inside Seguin's city limits and is locally known as the McKee site. Initial analysis suggests this was a major trading site.

Times changed dramatically with the arrival of the Spaniards after their 1521 conquest of Mexico. There were some 11 expeditions into Spanish Texas between 1689 and 1718. Two of these expeditions explored parts of today's Seguin and Guadalupe County. The first of these two expeditions in this region was that of Gov. Domingo Teran de los Rios in 1691 and 1692. Gov. Martin de Alarcon's 1718 expedition was the second. He was directed to establish a fort and a mission on the San Antonio River in present-day San Antonio. While construction was taking place, he sought routes to east Texas. Twice he passed through Guadalupe County, where his diarists remarked on flora, fauna, and river-crossing sites.

As Spain increased its discoveries and established settlements, they often used the Native American trade routes, such as those along the Guadalupe River. Eventually the Native Americans became messengers and postal carriers for the Spaniards as their communiqués with the missions and presidios of east Texas.

In 1825, Green DeWitt was granted a colony that included the present-day counties of Gonzales and Guadalupe. Following the Texas Revolution, the Anglo population quickly expanded. Available land for settlement around Gonzales became scarce. In 1838, Joseph Martin led a group of investors to the springs of Walnut Creek, some 36 miles west of Gonzales. These investors were mostly Texas Rangers and had seen duty throughout this western region of the DeWitt colony. Meeting under the Ranger Oaks, on August 12, 1838, these investors created Seguin (originally called Walnut Springs) on the hill leading down to the Guadalupe River.

Through these pre–Civil War years, businessmen, ranchers, farmers, teachers, and clergymen forged Seguin and Guadalupe County's identity. This identity has become one of multiculturalism. There were the German immigrants of the 1840s and 1850s who followed the German immigrant trail from Indianola through Seguin to New Braunfels and its gateway to the hill country.

Slavery in Seguin and Guadalupe County was practiced mostly in the rural areas, but also within Seguin. At one point, 32 percent of this area's population was slaves. After emancipation, many black colonies and communities appeared, thus maintaining their rich cultural heritage. Jakes Colony, Sweet Home Community, the Fennel Colony, Roosevelt School, and York Creek were some of these. Of historic interest are the Wilson pottery sites that were established by Hiram and James Wilson when the Civil War was over. Being granted the land by their white slave master John M. Wilson, these pottery sites became the first fully owned black business in the state of Texas.

The Hispanic community also remained and grew. In the early years, the Hispanic community experienced social disenfranchisement, as evidenced through their Mexican schools, such as Barbarossa and Juan Seguin. Throughout these years, they forged their culture and heritage through backbreaking labor on farms and ranches, small stores, personal farming, and ranching and education. Through *mutualistas*, or societies, churches, and ethnic pride, they emerged as strong, vibrant business and cultural contributors to the story of Seguin and Guadalupe County.

Although not along any of the great cattle drive trails to Kansas and beyond, Seguin certainly had its share of cattle drives to San Antonio and the first cattle drive to California by Michael Erskine in 1852. The 1870s railroad era saw Seguin and Guadalupe County having tracks from Houston to Luling through Seguin to Schertz-Cibolo and San Antonio. Also connecting Seguin to other regions in Texas are U.S. Highway 90 and U.S. Highway 3 (present-day U.S. Highway 90A). State Highway 123 north and south connects Seguin to Karnes City and San Marcos. State Highway 46 now terminates in Seguin and leads drivers through New Braunfels and the Hill Country of Boerne to Medina, Bandera, and Kerrville. In the 1960s, the U.S. Air Force added its auxiliary air training field on the east side of Seguin. At the same time, Interstate Highway 10 was built connecting San Antonio to Houston. By 2011, new State Highway 130, beginning near Georgetown, will terminate on Interstate Highway 10 five miles east of Seguin, thus bringing greater vehicular traffic into to this area.

Early businesses included mercantile stores, hardware stores, furniture makers, saloons, barbershops, meat markets, builders, and lodging for the drummers. Eventually a railed trolley line extended from the train depot to the county courthouse along Austin Street, bringing many visitors and businesses to downtown. Soon there were drugstores such as Burgess and Sergers alongside the family-owned stores that were so much a part of Seguin's vibrancy. Three major local banks were in full business by the early 20th century, Nolte Bank, First National Bank, and Citizens State Bank (Seguin State Bank), all providing needed services for the agricultural and business communities.

Education has always been a cornerstone of life throughout Seguin and Guadalupe County. County and city schools in the 1800s to mid-1900s dotted the landscape. So too did higher education: Guadalupe Colored College was established in 1884 and was the southernmost black Baptist college in the United States at that time. It was followed by a Lutheran college, which moved from Bryan to Seguin in 1911 and 1912. Today Texas Lutheran University is ranked as one of the leading academic small universities in the nation.

The business community has continuously evolved from its early mercantile stores of local brick companies; bakery shops, such as Keller's; Hey's Potato Chips; and Henry Troell, which provided the first hydroelectricity to Seguin to Hagan's cotton gins and the steel mill of Structural Metals, Inc. (CMC Steel-Texas). Today the business community includes national and international corporations such as Caterpillar, Hexcel, Alamo Industrial, CMC Steel-Texas, Tyson Foods, Continental, and Wal-Mart.

Seguin has been blessed with culture, educators, singers, writers, military veterans, ranchers and farmers, philanthropists, ministers, athletes, artists, and politicians at the local, state, and national levels. Its population trends reflect its promising future: In 1990, there were 18,553 Seguin citizens and 64,874 in Guadalupe County. In 2009, the city grew to more than 25,000 and the county topped 112,000.

One

PREHISTORIC AND HISTORIC SEGUIN

ENVIRONMENTAL AND HUMAN LEGACIES

Millions of years ago, where Seguin is today 14 miles south of New Braunfels, 36 miles east of San Antonio, and 36 miles west of Gonzales, the area was well underwater. It may have been an outer barrier reef of what today is the Gulf of Mexico, and the beaches would have been nestled along the southern and eastern borders of the Balcones Escarpment of the Hill Country.

It is not surprising that numerous fossils of saltwater marine life have been found, examined, and described by geologists, such as Dr. Evelyn Streng, now emeritus professor of geography at Texas Lutheran University. Following the receding oceans over the millennia were the ice ages. The last one was about 12,000 years ago. Wooly mastodons roamed through Seguin's environs, as did early horses, armadillos, and other like species. As the climate warmed, early humankind, in pursuit of wild game and grain, emerged in this region. Through the examination of artifacts, it is known that these indigenous peoples were here at least 8,000 years ago. Their extensive trail networks became the markers for the later explorations of the Spanish explorers, who chose San Antonio as their hub between San Juan Bautista along the Rio Grande below present-day Eagle Pass to the missions and presidios of east Texas.

Settling in this area were numerous Spanish, Mexican, and eventually Anglo, German, Polish, and African Americans, all leaving their marks on what today is Seguin, Guadalupe County, and south-central Texas. This book is their story that continues dynamically into the emerging 21st century.

Texas is blessed with numerous and beautiful rivers from the Sabine River in east Texas to the Rio Grande. Nestled in between is the Guadalupe River, whose origin is in the Balcones Escarpment near Kerrville. It meanders through Guadalupe County, where it is handed off to Gonzales County and receives the San Marcos River, continuing until it empties into the Gulf of Mexico.

Throughout its history, the Guadalupe River has sustained human and animal life. Numerous Native American campsites can be seen along or near the banks. The Guadalupe River was crossed by most of the Spanish expeditions into Texas and later by Texas revolutionists, Mexican armies, bandits, filibusters, cattlemen, ferries, cotton barges, and bridges too many to name.

The other major river in Guadalupe County is on the eastern boundary–the San Marcos River. Its origins are the Aquarena Springs in San Marcos, a major trading site for Native American tribes throughout northern Mexico, west Texas, and beyond to the lower Midwest and the southeastern United States. This gently flowing river meets the Guadalupe River near Gonzales.

Millions of years ago, this area of Texas was under the ocean. As the waters receded and the last ice age began to melt, treasures began to show themselves, including celephapods, sharks teeth, gastropods, and coral. As the ice age slowly warmed, wooly mammoths gave way to the early horse, armadillos, and other less furry or wooly animals. Shown here is a small sample of their many remains in Guadalupe County. (Courtesy of Stanley Naumann.)

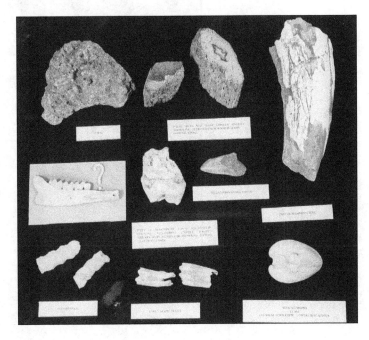

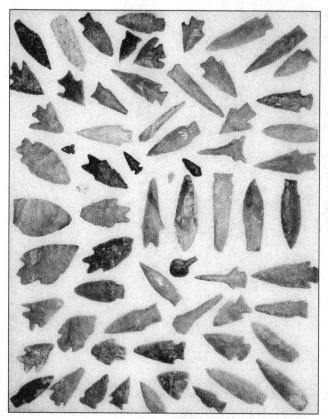

One of the many geographic features of Seguin and Guadalupe County's region was flint outcroppings or cores that appealed to the early Native Americans. By the time the Spaniards arrived, tribes had developed an extensive trail network from the coast to well into the hill country along these rivers. In this photograph are awls, gouges, spearheads, and points for bird hunting. The knowledgeable collector will be amazed at the tools represented here. (Courtesy of Stanley Naumann.)

There was plenty of activity along the Geromino Creek, so named by the Spaniards in honor of St. Jerome. Some of these artifacts date to 6,500 BC, or roughly 8,500 years ago. These are evidenced by the Angostura dart point. Also evidenced is the high degree of ingenuity of these earliest indigenous inhabitants by their practical inventiveness, such as sinkers for a throw line net to catch fish. (Courtesy of Bob Everett.)

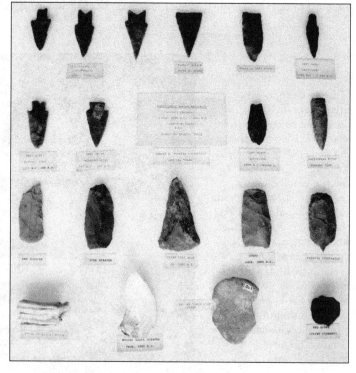

This collection, found by Floyd and Jody McKee inside Seguin's city limits and along the Guadalupe River, reflects the apparent need of the early Native Americans for scraping tools and gouges. This indicates an abundance of game, big and small, as well as a tendency, at least at this location, for a more sedentary way of life. (Courtesy of Stanley Naumann.)

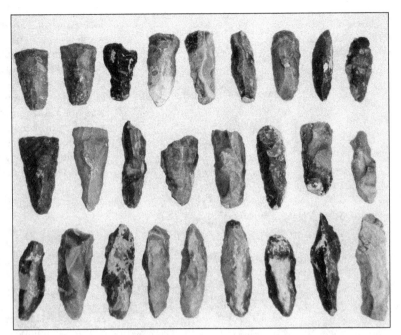

To the casual observer, this photograph shows a bunch of broken pieces of something. But they are actually shards of broken pottery. The Spaniards, at their major crossing point below Eagle Pass and Guerrero, Coahuila, Mexico, had established several missions and employed and trained many different groups of Native Americans, who were taught pottery making. These skills were passed on to San Antonio and to the missions into east Texas. (Courtesy of Stanley Naumann.)

Jose Antonio Navarro was one of three Mexicans to sign the Texas Declaration of Independence from Mexico. His family was influential in early San Antonio, and they were close friends of Erasmo Seguin and his family. It was not a surprise that Navarro and Juan Seguin became close friends. The Navarro ranch was in what is now Guadalupe County along the Geronimo Creek near present-day Geronimo.

Archaeological steward Bob Everett of the Guadalupe County Historical Commission excavated the Navarro ranch house. A number of artifacts are shown in the next several photographs that offer an insight to life in the 1700s and early 1800s in the Seguin and Guadalupe County area.

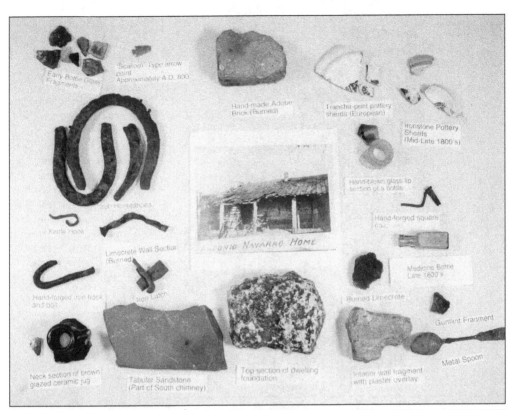

Early Bottle Glass Fragments

"Scallorn" Type arrow point Approximately A.D. 800

Hand-made Adobe Brick (Burned)

Transfer-print pottery sherds (European)

Ironstone Pottery Sherds (Mid-Late 1800's)

Iron Horseshoes

Kettle Hook

Limecrete Wall Section (Burned)

Hand-blown glass lip section of a bottle

Hand-forged square nail

Medicine Bottle Late 1800's

Hand-forged iron hook and bolt

Iron Latch

Burned Limecrete

Gunflint Fragment

Neck section of brown glazed ceramic jug

Tabular Sandstone (Part of South chimney)

Top section of dwelling foundation

Interior wall fragment with plaster overlay

Metal Spoon

ANTONIO NAVARRO HOME

As the western civilization moved into this south-central Texas region, a mixing of cultures evolved. At top left is a small arrow flanked by an early glass bottle and transfer print pottery from Europe. Iron artifacts for practical daily use, such as horseshoes, a door latch, and a kettle hook, entered as indigenous tools disappeared. Replacing the early Native American dwellings of cane, brush, and foliage were adobe structures. (Courtesy of Stanley Naumann.)

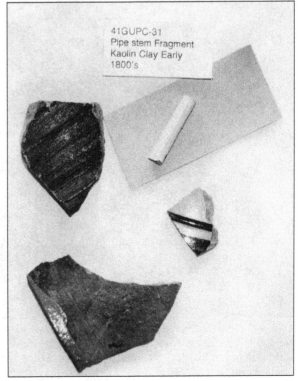

41GUPC-31
Pipe stem Fragment
Kaolin Clay Early
1800's

Shown here is a remnant of an early-19th-century clay pipe stem near the Navarro ranch site. Whether these artifacts were Mexican, Anglo, or Native American is incidental to the increased evidence of an emerging and more modern way of life. (Courtesy of Stanley Naumann.)

This clay Mexican bean pot was located at the Navarro site with many other artifacts. Upon closer scrutiny, notice that the outside had a dull finish while the inside was much shinier. It was probably used for storage as well as cooking. On the lower-to-middle levels on the outside, it is easy to see the smoky remnants of the fires this pot must have been perched on. (Courtesy of Stanley Naumann.)

This is the only known photograph of the Manuel Flores house. Juan Seguin married into the Flores family, who were ranchers near present-day Floresville. Flores's house was on the Guadalupe River. He began building a dam across the river that today is the known as the Saffold Dam by Starcke Park.

This is the end result of what Flores started with his dam across the Guadalupe River. It was completed in the late 1800s by William Saffold and became the site of Seguin's hydroelectric plant. The dam was named after Saffold completed his work. It is called the Saffold Dam.

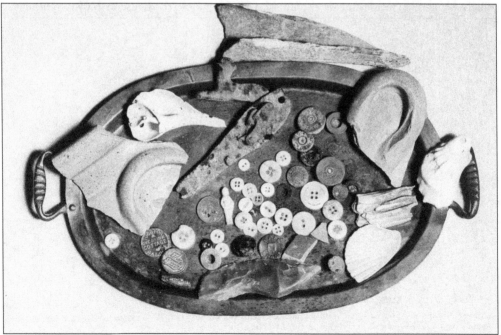

As the Spaniards began to explore Texas in earnest in the late 1500s through the 1700s, more evidence of western life emerges from archaeological discoveries, as well as what present-day landowners uncover or discount. In this photograph from the McKee site, saltwater shells are seen along with more modern artifacts of the 19th century. (Courtesy of Stanley Naumann.)

William Saffold built the Saffold-Blanks-McKee house in 1865. Saffold owned an entire league in the Eligio Gortari grant (over 4,400 acres). Neither he nor Manuel Flores or Will Blanks knew they were living on the largest prehistoric Native American trading site south of the San Marcos–Aquarena Springs site. Jody and Floyd McKee bought the house in 2005 to restore it.

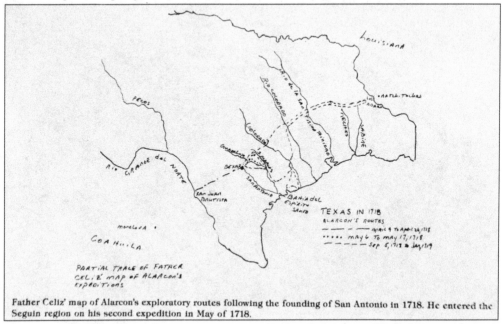

Father Celiz' map of Alarcon's exploratory routes following the founding of San Antonio in 1718. He entered the Seguin region on his second expedition in May of 1718.

This is a copy of the author's basic interpretation of Father Celiz's map of Gov. Martín Alarcón's expedition into this area between 1718 and 1719. Note that part of his expedition explored between the San Marcos and Guadalupe Rivers, as well as Geronimo Creek. It is through Celiz's accounts that readers learn of the early flora and fauna of this region. (Courtesy of Stanley Naumann.)

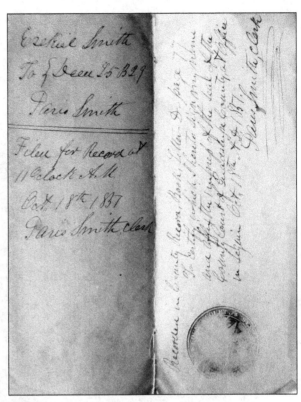

The next two photographs are of an 1837 deed transaction for Ezekiel Smith and Paris Smith. Although Seguin was not established until August 12, 1838, the early investors, led by Joseph Martin of Gonzales, were conducting transactions for early purchases of the land that eventually became the city of Seguin. In this transaction, Paris Smith is purchasing lot No. 6 of block No. 29 in the Seguin inner-town lots. Later he built a house on this site. The cost of the lot was $25. Soon the cost of inner-city lots dramatically increased. (Both, courtesy of Stanley Naumann.)

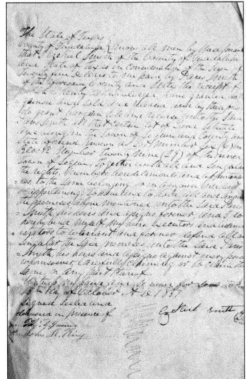

This photograph of French Smith appeared in an unidentified newspaper that was passed on to his descendents. He had a distinguished career as a captain in the Texas Rangers and fought in numerous battles, including the ones after the Texas Revolution against Gen. Rafael Vázquez and later Gen. Adrian Woll's attempts to retake San Antonio and bring it under Mexican control. (Courtesy of Stanley Naumann.)

Two

Foundations of
Early Seguin
Beginnings of a New Era

Seguin was officially founded on August 12, 1838, by its small group of investors. Most of the 33 were Texas Rangers who had served during the prerevolutionary period through the Texas Revolution and continued to do so during and after the republic was founded. Names like Jack Coffee Hayes, Ben McCulloch, Moses Campbell, William King, and French Smith were just a few among many.

Their task was formidable. The steps they took determined the town's destiny and longevity. They apparently did well, for Seguin will celebrate its 175th anniversary in 2013, but it was not an easy task. It was truly a frontier town almost equidistant between San Antonio and Gonzales. The original road into Seguin was south of the Guadalupe River. It sprung north from the San Antonio–Gonzales road basically along present-day Farm-to-Market Road 466 and Farm-to-Market Road 477. Today that road is named Austin Street, or State Highway 123 Business.

After originally naming the town Walnut Springs, the founders learned there was another community so named. Gathering under the Ranger Oaks among the springs of Walnut Branch (locally referred to as Walnut Creek), they voted to name the town in honor of Juan Seguin, a hero of the Texas Revolution and eventually a senator to the young Republic of Texas.

Once they organized themselves, a map was drawn dividing the community into four sections. There were the inner town lots, the timber and river lots, the acre lots, and the farming lots. In the downtown lots, the two center blocks were to always be accessible to the public. They remain so today. On one block is the Guadalupe County Courthouse; the city square is the other block, located directly south of the courthouse with Center Street (today's Donegan Street) separating the two inner-city blocks. These two blocks remain the focal point of all the city's major celebrations today: the Fourth of July parade and Freedom Fiesta, the Christmas parade and Holiday Stroll, Cinco de Mayo, Fiestas Patrias, Diez y Seis, and numerous concerts and related activities.

The founders also placed a heavy emphasis on education, religious worship, and a sound business environment. These foundations of the community continue to this day, although there is much more to enjoy on a daily basis.

This picture is of Juan Seguin during his early years as a colonel in the Texas army. He cut a dashing figure and was a zealous fighter for independence. He fought at the Alamo until William B. Travis dispatched him to seek reinforcements. Seguin was a mayor of San Antonio and a senator in the second session of the young republic's government. (Courtesy of Stanley Naumann.)

Walnut Creek is located just east of Guadalupe Street and south of Court Street. It was near this location that the early founders of Seguin met to lay out the plans for the town in 1838. The springs still flow to this day, and the area is as beautiful as it was 172 years ago.

On the west bank of the springs and Walnut Creek was a rustic ranger station that also served as Seguin's first hospital. It was here that Susan Calvert met her future husband, Jack Coffee Hays, who was a distinguished ranger throughout central Texas. Dorothy Jarmon remembers living in this building with her parents, four sisters, and brother in the mid-1940s.

Although these are not the original Texas Rangers who settled early Seguin, this group did serve in this area in either the late 1800s or early 1900s. Among those pictured are, from left to right, (first row) Tipper Harris, Johnny Rogers, Capt. James "John" Brooks, and Charles Rogers; (second row) Arren Rogers (third from left).

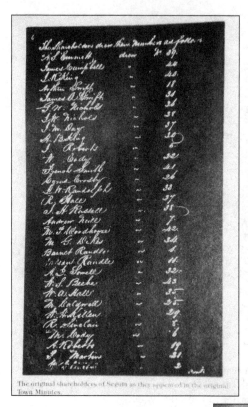

The original shareholders of Seguin as they appeared in the original Town Minutes.

The 33 early investors, led by Joseph S. Martin, were talented, shrewd, and frontier toughened. They had served in the Texas Revolution, and many continued on as Texas Rangers. French Smith was elected as the president, with James Campbell, John Russell, John Gray, George Nichols, and Michael Cody in charge of laying out the city.

Dated in 1849, this agreement between homeowner Paris Smith and builder A. M. Boyd was a contract to build Smith's home. The dimensions of the home had to meet the first building codes in Seguin: It had to be no less than "16' square with an entrance to be covered 14' at one end of said building."

One of Seguin's early founders was Asa Sowell. His home was not inside the inner-city blocks but was about one-quarter mile away in the timber lots on a hill looking over Seguin, where today's Seguin Housing Authority is located. The Gordon family later added on to the original Sowell home.

The Campbell-Hoermann log cabin is now located on East Washington Street on the Seguin Conservation Society's Heritage Village. It is representative of the cabins in early Guadalupe County in the 1840s. It was originally mud caulked during the winter months and uncaulked between the logs during the spring to fall months. Originally it was a one-room cabin but was expanded in later years to include a kitchen and dog run.

This mid- to late-1800s photograph shows the county's first of four courthouses. It was located on the 100 block of East Court Street and North River Street directly across the street from the public square, where the remaining three courthouses were later built. Eventually this became the John Hey building.

This stately native live oak tree next to the Plaza Hotel on the north corner of East Nolte and South River Streets and directly across the street from market square, or central park, was the "hanging tree." The legend is that Susan Calvert, who was being courted by Texas Ranger Jack Coffee Hays, was riding along the banks of the Guadalupe River and was assailed but broke away. Her fiancé, Hays, found the culprit, brought him back to Seguin, and hung him from this tree.

William G. King is pictured with his wife, Euphemia Texas Davis Ashley King, and dog Peaches. He was one of the founders of Seguin. They were married in 1850 in the forerunner of today's First United Methodist Church, and he became influential in Seguin's early development while serving as a Texas Ranger and community organizer. For many years, he was the county clerk for Seguin and Guadalupe County.

One of Seguin's most enduring and fabled stores across from the market and public square was the Vivroux Hardware Store. This store was founded in 1869 by Phillip Vivroux and continued until it was destroyed by fire in 2001. It was a mainstay in Seguin for all people near and far, and it always had hardware parts for those patrons who recycled everything.

A number of ferries developed along the river to shuttle people with their horses, donkeys, and produce from one side to the other. Most ferries were for farmers, who were pulled across the river on a cable. This ferry was located near present-day CMC Steel-Texas, the site of the former Seguin Flour Mill and Structural Metals, Inc. (SMI).

Located on the southeast corner of East Court and South River Streets directly across from the central square or park and the second courthouse was the Bergfeld Drug Store. In the foreground are the trolley tracks of the downtown mule-drawn trolley car. The German language signs mixed with English reflect the ancestry of many of the Anglo settlers and business establishments in early downtown Seguin.

The C. H. Harris store was located at 100 West Court Street on the north side. Today it is Pat Irvine King's Law Office. F. H. Harris owned and operated the store (standing in the foreground, left) while his son Britt (standing in the foreground, right), assisted him. Pictured between them is Britt's daughter.

The *Seguin Enterprise* was originally on the 100 block of South River Street and occupied the office of Seguin's first newspaper, the 1853 *Seguin Mercury*. The *Seguin Enterprise* was eventually located on North Austin Street across from the second and third courthouses. Of all of Seguin's numerous newspapers, this one continues reporting Seguin-area news as the *Seguin Gazette-Enterprise*. The *Seguin Enterprise* published the original John Wesley Hardin autobiography.

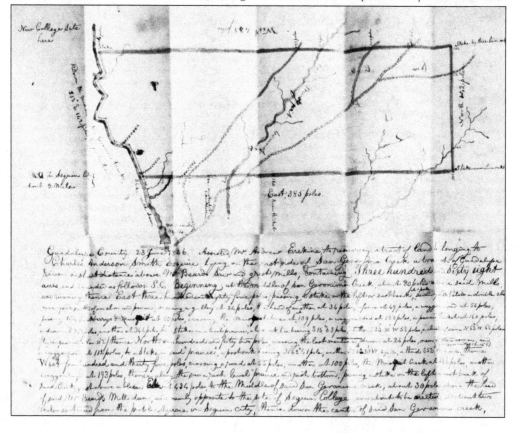

Estate planning was not uncommon on the frontier in 1846. These two photographs reflect Charles A. Smith's concern in passing to his heirs his 368-acre ranch along the Geronimo Creek 2 miles north of Seguin. The map provided interesting measurements used by the surveyors at that time.

Shown in this 1891 picture is an example of the expanding businesses along South Austin Street across from the two inner-city blocks. Pictured are the Will Blanks store (left) and the John Ireland building. Across Center Street is the more modern Vivroux Hardware Store. The Masonic lodge met on its second floor in the mid-1800s.

The Seguin Fire Department was established in 1877. This 1883 photograph by C. L. Hickson shows Seguin's first fire department building, located on the southeast corner of Austin and Gonzales Streets in 1883. From left to right are Hy Bartholomae, Steve Gallagher, unidentified, Ralph Parish, two unidentified, A. G. Swope, two unidentified, Paul Goetz, Watt Simmons, two unidentified, Ferdinand Klein, unidentified, D. E. Pelly, unidentified, and Will Vickers. They pumped water from a well at the courthouse square to fill their pumper tanks.

This home, locally known as the Matthies house, was built by Union Civil War veteran Maj. Alexander Moore in 1879 in the sand hills southeast of Seguin. It remains in the family today and is used on a regular basis. The stately balconies and porches were added in 1908 by Fred Matthies but later were removed. (Courtesy of Fred Blumberg.)

Mentioned earlier was John Ireland, a colorful and prominent lawyer in Seguin in the mid-19th century. He served as a state representative from 1872 to 1874 and in the senate from 1874 to 1876. He was governor in 1882, during which time the state capitol was built.

It has been said in Seguin that there were as many churches as there were saloons. Although this has never been proven, Seguin did have its share of saloons and was always ready to have a parade or celebration. Eddie Fiegerle (right) is standing in front of Schultz' Saloon, facing Court Street. He was a saloon keeper, and judging by his attire, he ran a well-respected establishment.

Vaudeville entertainment was immensely popular in Seguin. Their venues of entertainment were opera houses, usually located on the second floor of downtown buildings. The Klein Opera House was located in the 1880 C. E. Tips building on the southwest corner of Austin and Court Streets. The first floor was the hardware store. Today's owner is Robert Raetzsch.

In the early 1850s, Dr. John E. Park developed limecrete, which dramatically changed house building in Seguin and Guadalupe County. This limecrete structure is known as Sebastopol. The families of Col. Joshua Young and later Joseph Zorn were involved in Sebastopol's building. The Koehler Construction Company, in coordination with the Texas Department of Parks and Wildlife, restored Sebastopol in the 1980s as a state park.

Throughout Seguin's history, concerts in the downtown square have been an integral part of the city's culture. The bands were well organized and brought huge crowds as they played in the bandstand (often called the gazebo by locals). One such early band was this Central Park Band, active from 1890 to 1900. Their music was light and certainly uplifting during this period of the Victorian era.

By 1876, Seguin acquired a more modern means of transportation—the railroad. By then, the Buffalo Bayou, Brazos, and Colorado Railway had changed its name to the Galveston, Harrisburg, and San Antonio Railway and had laid tracks from Luling to San Antonio, with a station in Seguin. This new depot became an integral part of Seguin's economic development in the late 1800s through the late 1900s.

This collage of Rev. William Baton Ball, although dated 1909, reflects his life in the 1800s. He served in the Union during the Civil War, later becoming a buffalo soldier and then an educator. He was instrumental in establishing education for black children in 1871, as well as the Abraham Lincoln School, which eventually became Ball High School. He was also president of Guadalupe College.

In 1884, the black Baptists established a school on the site of where the Joe F. Saegert sixth-grade campus now stands (previously the Seguin High School and middle school) on North Travis Street. By 1887, it was recognized as the Guadalupe Colored College (later called Guadalupe College) and eventually moved to its present site west of Seguin on U.S. Highway 90. This photograph shows its original location near downtown Seguin.

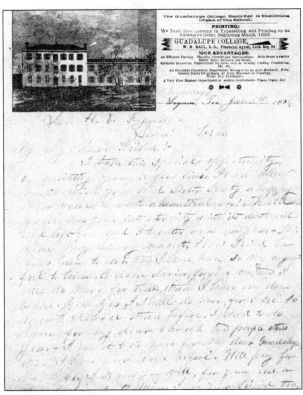

As president of Guadalupe College, Ball corresponded with numerous friends and colleagues. This handwritten letter is photographed from its original, which is on display in Seguin's heritage museum. The letterhead gives a good view of the college at its relocated site on West Court Street and an insight to Ball's desires to do well as its president. Ball's efforts led to Guadalupe College's expansion in the vocational fields. By doing so, many of its graduates went on to become teachers, independent farmers, ranchers, and business leaders.

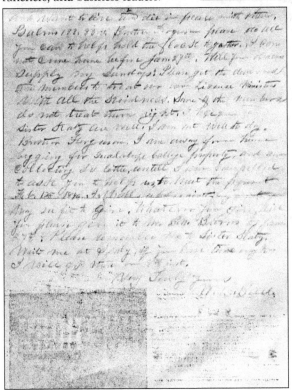

VATER MUTTER

OTTO
HEINEMEYER
GEB.
MARZ 24, 1864
GEST.
JAN. 12, 1893

Alles in der Natur
stirbt und lebt.
Nichts ist auf
immer todt.

ANNA
HEINEMEYER
GEB.
JAN. 7, 1869
GEST.
NOV. 28, 1892

Unsers Daseins
schlummernde Gebeine,
Hüllt das Dunkel
der Vergangenheit.

HEINEMEYER

The German immigrants who settled in Seguin and Guadalupe County from the 1840s to the 1860s left a proud heritage. Although the German language is no longer one of the main languages due to social factors, German contributions remain visible to all. This headstone, inscribed in German, reflects the pride and attention to detail the Germans so enjoyed.

Three

BUSINESSES, AGRICULTURE, AND POLITICS
19TH AND EARLY 20TH CENTURIES

The foundations Seguin established in its formative years were solid. The very infrastructure of Seguin remains to this day in terms of its political system, government, public safety, religious toleration, sound education, recreation, business, and commerce. There also continues to be a close relationship between the city and county governments.

The period from 1840 to 1940 witnessed an evolutionary process in community development that reflects Seguin's ongoing cultural history to this day and certainly into the future. Soon after Seguin's founding, church services no longer needed to be held in family homes. Buildings sprung up around the two inner-city blocks along Court Street, Austin Street, Nolte Street, and River Street and to points north, south, east, and west of the town's center. Politicians met in the first courthouse on the corner of East Court Street and North River Street until slaves built the stately second courthouse in 1857 on the public square just across the street. Two subsequent courthouses have been built on the same site in 1889 and 1936. By 1852, a strong mayor–city council government was established, later to be replaced by the city manager form of government in 1986.

Roads expanded, increasing commerce from Seguin, with the arrival of new German immigrants in New Braunfels, the birth of San Marcos, and its historic relations with Gonzales and San Antonio. Numerous agricultural communities in Guadalupe County emerged with their own churches and schools, including Elm Creek, Zuehl, Fentress, Dowdy, Olmos, O'Daniel, and Post Oak, but they still traded in Seguin. Many still remain in the county.

There were many changes. A postal system emerged, as did cotton gins and corn silos. The railroad and its depot came in the 1870s, connecting Seguin to Houston and San Antonio. Men and horses joined Theodore Roosevelt in the Spanish-American War. Some citizens became state politicians, and bridges began to replace the ferries.

These years were not always easy. There were recessions, failed banking systems, and drought. Yet a strong work ethic and faith in self, community, and God strongly forged and became a lasting characteristic of Seguin and its environs.

National Baseball Hall of Famer "Smokey" Joe Williams is seen in this photograph walking across Court Street at the corner of Austin Street with his nephew tagging along. The photograph was taken before 1908 because First National Bank was not yet built. Williams was inducted into the National Baseball Hall of Fame in 1999, alongside fellow Texan Nolan Ryan.

Texas Rangers Co. A., 1910

(1) A.J.Sowell; (2)S.T.Townsend; (3) Charley Pace; (4)Joe Davenport; (5) S.Smiley; (6) A.R.Baker; (7) Robt.Speed; (8) Sam M°Kenzie; (9)Capt.J.J.Sanders;(10)Earl Yeary.

Although the frontier was disappearing in the late 1800s and early 1900s, Texas Rangers were still needed. The first ranger on the left is A. J. Sowell, a descendent of one of Seguin's founders. This 1910 photograph of Texas Rangers, Company A, is believed to have been taken, appropriately so, under the Ranger Oaks on West Gonzales Street.

Ezra Keyser built Guadalupe County's second courthouse in 1857 on the south side of Court Street on the public square. It replaced the wooden structure on the corner of North River and Court Streets. Since 1857, two successive courthouses were constructed on the same site. The laborers for the second courthouse were slaves. Many slaves were sold, mortgaged, or hired for labor on the front steps of this courthouse.

This cotton wagon is seen in front of the third courthouse, built in 1889, and is being pulled by a team of bulls and cows. The team masters are believed to be former slaves, who, among many former slaves, took their former owners names and began a new era as freedmen following emancipation and the Reconstruction era. Even to this day, cotton remains a viable crop in Guadalupe County.

Mrs. Leonard Merriweather was a former slave. Here she is surrounded by four of her grandsons with the Capote Hills in the far distance. There were several plantations in neighboring Comal/Guadalupe County along present-day Highway 46 between New Braunfels and Clear Springs. German immigrant Heinrich Timmermann learned English from slaves when he worked on a Comal County plantation and spoke with the Gullah accent the rest of his life.

As agriculture was well developed throughout Guadalupe County, many of the farmers needed seasonal help for planting and harvests. Local *troqueros*, or truckers, had labor contracts with the owners and ferried many Hispanic families to and from the Seguin barrios. Pictured here is the Elizendo family on their way to work. (Courtesy of Ramón Salazar Jr.)

The Flores-Saffold Dam gained its greatest moment in local history when it became the generator for Seguin's first electrical power in 1908. Local entrepreneur Henry Troell was the guiding light for creating what became Seguin's power plant long before the Rural Electric Agency came to the nation's rural communities in the 1930s. The power plant is still located at this site.

Troell, with wife, Johanna, is pictured here with 10 of their children. Troell also built several gins and the two-story Troell building at 114 North River Street in 1898. This building had an opera house on the second floor and four separate businesses on the first floor. Today it is the Seguin heritage museum.

As Seguin had its hanging tree across from market square, it also had its whipping tree on market square. Prisoners were brought to the square on Saturdays, and as public punishment, the sheriff had the guilty person publicly whipped. The tree is still there.

In the early years, Guadalupe County and Seguin's political structure reflected the size of its rural constituency. The 1900–1904 commissioners' court was presided over by county judge F. C. Weinert, who later became an influential state senator. Pictured below, from left to right, are commissioner ? Lillard, commissioner ? Erck, ? Weinert, unidentified, and ? Gosemann.

Cotton was still king of the crops in the early 20th century. An Avery truck driven by Alfred Koebig of Geronimo pulled this load of 39 bales. He also owned Koebig's store in Geronimo, which housed that town's first post office. Like many rural families, the Koebigs engaged in the mercantile sector as well as agriculture.

Jugend-Verein der Tabor-Gemeinde zu Cottonwood.

Many of the rural communities retained their cultural identity well into the 20th century. One of these, Cottonwood, was predominantly German. The citizens were highly organized and proud of their younger generation, who were taking their destiny into the future, as evidenced by youth organizations and leaders in this photograph. Many went on to become successful in the agricultural business world.

Conrad's photographic studio was in downtown Seguin. This hearty group of gentlemen, pictured in April 1903, included staunch businessmen not only in downtown Seguin, but in the county as well. From left to right are (first row) H. Oelkers and Lee Jones; (second row) ? Engelke, Harry Wurzbach, A. Seidemann, and J. Kuhnert; (third row) ? Stokes, ? Krueger, and A. Leissner.

The First National Bank was built in 1908, but it was in business prior to that date and was located in the C. E. Tips building. In 1907, Charles Tips was made cashier. Pictured here from left to right are unidentified, Tips, R. W. Erck (cashier), and C. C. Dibrell (bookkeeper). Today the Tips building, on the southwest corner of Court and Austin Streets, is owned by Robert Raetzsch.

Seguin's first formal post office was established around 1920 at the corner of South Austin and Nolte Streets, and it was inside the Nolte Bank. From left to right are A. A. Vordenbaum, postmaster; Theo Hoffmann, city carrier; Will Vickers, rural carrier; and Henry Koch, clerk. Up until this time, the post office was wherever a government contract was let, be it a barbershop, a haberdashery, or a vacant building.

Seguin's first mail car was this hand-carved, wooden two-seater with spoked wheels that traveled the streets of Seguin and surrounding nearby communities, such as McQueeney, Elm Creek, and Mill Creek. More often than not flat tires and muddy roads delayed the mail, but those incidents never stopped it from being delivered.

By 1935, Seguin's postal system had gone from James Campbell's 1839 appointment as postmaster to John Neill in 1846 and then to his daughter Caledonia Neill Baxter, who first ran it out of a tree house next to Nolte Bank and then from this 1935 permanent structure. On the steps, from left to right, are D. D. Baker, F. C. Weinert, H. H. Weinert, Max Starcke, and C. H. Donegan.

Geronimo also has a postal history, with its first postmaster appointed in 1886. As seen in this photograph, it was located in Alfred Koebig's store. Melitta Timmermann was one of its most loyal clerks over the years when she worked for Koebig, Louis Heinemeyer, Annie Heinemeyer, and Elva Harborth.

Throughout its history, Seguin has enjoyed bringing the community together. In 1922, close to the present fairgrounds, an amusement park was set up to treat young and old to the new rides that were popular in the more urban areas of Texas and the United States. This early merry-go-round was obviously popular.

It is unknown when the first parades began in Seguin or who the organizers were. What is known is that they began in the 1800s, and the courthouse on the public square and the city park have since been the focal point of parade routes. Most parades have historically begun on North Austin Street and ended on South Austin Street. Today Seguin enjoys numerous parades throughout the year.

The 1853 *Seguin Mercury* was the city's first newspaper, located in the 100 block of South River Street. There were a number of other newspapers, including the German language *Seguin Zeitung*. Shown in this 1909 parade photograph, the *Seguin Enterprise* won second place and $7.50. From left to right are Joe Goetz, James Calvert (manager), Jay Calvert, Cora G. Smith (publisher), Edgar Petry, Earl Reid, Leonard K. McDaniel, and Jesse McKee.

Shown in this 1906 Fourth of July parade photograph are youngsters dressed up as Buster Browns, celebrating the Buster Brown shoes that were so popular into the 1940s. H. A. Ernst and Brothers sponsored the float. The children are pictured on North Austin Street next to the third courthouse after finishing the parade.

The Davenport Butcher Shop was one of four businesses located in the 1898 Troell building on North River Street. Iron posts that still stand in the building separated the four shops, and they supported makeshift walls separating the stores. There were staircases in the front and rear of the building leading to the second floor.

THE KEMPENSTEIN THEATRE

ONE NIGHT ONLY
SAT. MAR. 28

GRAND OPENING OF
SEGUIN'S NEW THEATRE

Special engagement of The
Orpheum Vaudeville Co.
Headed by George Austin
Moore and seven other star
feature acts.

PRICES, 50c, 75c and $1.00

Upstairs in the Troell building was the Kempenstein Opera House. There was an alleyway on the south side of the building that led to a livery stable, and the stage actually extended over the alley. The vaudeville actors enjoyed performing in the early 1900s at the local opera houses. The stage was also used for high school graduations from the Mary B. Erskine School in the 1920s. These advertisements appeared in the *Seguin Enterprise*.

KEMPENSTEIN OPERA HOUSE

MONDAY, OCTOBER 19TH. 1908.

DELAVOYE & FRITS. Comedians

THE BIG CITY SHOW

THE AERIAL TWINS

SENSATIONAL AERIAL GYMNASTS

Popular Prices 15c, 25c and 35c

Reserved Seats At BURGES & WEINERTS Drug Store.

SALE OPENS SATURDAY MORNING.

S. White built the third courthouse in 1889, and A. F. Giles was the architect. The building was a blending of the second courthouse with the third. Balconies were added, and the new courthouse was raised higher. It took on more of a Victorian look than the plantation house style of the second courthouse, and the cupola became more pronounced. The present courthouse replaced it in 1938.

Seguin has experienced some spectacular fires in its downtown history. Perhaps one of the greatest fires was on May 3, 1907, when four buildings on Court Street directly across from the courthouse were destroyed. From left to right are the Krezdorn, Bruns, Fritz, and Hey buildings. The Hey building was originally the first county courthouse.

When these stores were reconstructed, the Fritz and Hey buildings on the east end were converted to single-story structures. Recently Bobby Schnuriger, a local builder, restored those two structures to look just as they did in this 1908 photograph. The stores continue to be occupied and conduct business as usual right across the street from the fourth courthouse.

Trade Days used to be called the farmers market. Originally local producers met every Saturday on the city square behind the courthouse. As can be seen by this news release in the *Seguin Enterprise*, the Seguin Fire Department had become an integral part of downtown celebrations. There were poultry exhibitions, livestock shows, and a grand parade, all bringing the city and county together.

Third Trades Day!
AND SEGUIN FIREMEN'S
Annual Celebration !
THURSDAY, MAY 4th, 1905.

Biggest Joint Celebration ever Held in Seguin. More People, More Music, More Attractions, More to See, More Good Chances to have a Good Time.

All exhibits, including the Poultry Department, but excluding all other live stock, should be in the Exhibition hall (the LeGette building formerly used by Felix Klappenbach) by 10 o'clock on the morning of April 20. All live stock should be hitched around the square. Space will be reserved for this purpose.

Grand Parade at 2 o'clock P. M. with Eberhard's Military Band, Fire Department, Decorated Hose Carts, Trucks, Carriages, Buggies, Bicycles, Etc.

Parade will start at Fire-House. Officers of Fire Department will be installed at grand stand in City Park by Mayor Zorn. Several fine speeches will be made. Firemen's races at 4 o'clock. Grand ball at night in Klein's hall. Amusement all day. Exhibits for competition accepted from Guadalupe and adjoining counties. All town people may exhibit, but will receive no premiums. Judging begins at 10 o'clock a. m. Secretary's office will be in exhibition hall. The secretary will list no exhibits for competition, heads of departments will accept same. Competitors for premiums given by firms and individuals must notify the secretary.

THEO. KOCH, President.
A. V. STEIN, Secretary.

To farmer bringing best coun- | pair President suspenders, Mis- | riding whip, Theo. Koch & Son;

One of the popular avenues for young boys to be members of the fire department was to first become a "heel fly." These youngsters were given this nickname by P. J. "Pick" Burgess because an increasing number of them began hanging around the firemen and were soon called heel flies. Usually they were 10 to 14 years old and were devout followers of their mentors. Many eventually became firemen.

With the advent of cars came the advent of gasoline stations. This Texaco station, although no longer providing gasoline, still stands as a garage at the Four Corners today at the intersection of North Austin and Kingsbury Streets (U.S. Highway 90). Four Corners remains a bustling site for automobile repairs, gasoline, and food purchases at Wuest's, Inc., Pic n' Pac store, one of a chain of Pic n' Pac stores..

One of the popular feed stores in the 1930s was the White House Poultry and Stock Feed store. Pictured from left to right are Charles Steinman (manager), Paul Willmann, a Mr. Deason (customer), Reno Moltz, Hugo Winsauer, Van Frein (kneeling), and unidentified. Today there are fewer feed stores in Seguin, but those that continue remain vital to the agriculture sector.

Ella Dibrell gracefully attended to this elegant parlor. Her family's two-story Victorian home was located on North River Street before the present-day city hall replaced the house. Dibrell was the founder of the Women's Federated Club of Seguin and a collector of Elisabeth Ney's remarkable sculptures. Two of those gracing the parlor were of Sam Houston and Stephen F. Austin.

In its formative years, Seguin was self-sufficient. The people grew their own food, and walnut trees, pecan trees, river cypress, and oak trees provided the wood for building. Businesses provided the practical daily needs. Brick making became one of the local industries, with companies opening, such as the Sonka Brick Factory on Guadalupe Street, Blumberg Bricks, homemade adobe brick outfits, and the McQueeney brick yard (pictured above). Today it is the Acme Brick Company.

The Women's Federated Club building, led by Ella Dibrell, was established on August 10, 1902. Representatives from three of the women's clubs met at Klein's Opera House (in the Tips building) to come up with a way for securing a restroom and a clubroom. Such a motion was made by a Mrs. Meyers. It was unanimously approved, and the captains of the Fat and Lean baseball teams offered to play two games with all the proceeds going to the club. Today all four of the women's clubs, the Seguin Shakespeare Club, the Seguin Study Club, the Delphian Literary Club, and the Tejas Literary Club, meet in the same building that has the clubroom and a restroom.

The Thad Miller Bridge replaced the old Saffold Ferry just about a quarter-mile below the Saffold Dam. A temporary floating bridge spanned the river until Miller built his bridge, a single-span structure that served Seguin well until the more modern F. C. Weinert Bridge was constructed in 1938.

When the train depot was built along the railroad tracks on North Austin Street and present-day Braden Street, businesses soon developed along North Austin Street to greet the travelers. Until the Seguin trolley car came into being, wagons took the visitors downtown, and passersby could shop at Hugo Starcke's store or just stop in at Eddie Feigerle's (pictured above, with a mustache) saloon for quick refreshment served by Louis Haberle (on left).

Not only was the new bridge built around 1938 and Starcke Park was becoming a reality, but also the fourth and present-day courthouse and today's city hall were being constructed. City hall was built on the site of the Ella Dibrell house. Pictured in this 1935 photograph was Mayor Max Starcke with councilmen and city workers. Starcke is under the painting of Juan Seguin.

Much of the construction in the 1930s could not have been done without the Civilian Conservation Corps (CCC). The CCC camp was just south of Starcke Park and the Weinert Bridge. In this aerial photograph, the view is to the north. The new bridge can be seen in the upper left, and Starcke Park is to its left. The old Seguin Airport grass runway is at the bottom of the photograph.

George Hagn (in the dark uniform in the center) led the 1935 Seguin Municipal Band. Instruments played included clarinets, trombones, saxophones, French horns, drums, tubas, and trumpets. Many community leaders were members of the band. Some of those pictured here are Eugene C. Dietert (clarinet), Bruno Dietert (French horn), Harry Schmidt (clarinet), Albert Springs (tuba), and Chester Schwab (drums). (Courtesy of Gene Dietert).

Trying to haul a load of cotton on an early Farmall tractor is Wayne Lange in the Laubach community of Guadalupe County. Cotton continues to be one of the rotating crops throughout the blackland prairie region of central Guadalupe County to this day. The Laubach community remains one of Guadalupe County's rich agricultural regions.

Four

School Days
and Churches
Then and Now

Schools and churches have historically been two of the bonding forces at the heart of Seguin and Guadalupe County's development. Other institutions that have bonded this region are the agricultural industries, banking industries, commercial businesses, and, in the latter part of the 20th century, manufacturing.

Seguin has often been referred to as a conservative community. Perhaps, if this is defined as being culturally and commercially so, then yes, this region has been steady yet progressive in its planning and successful in the long term. Seguin continues to have downtown as its heart; its recreational areas, especially along the Guadalupe River and the San Marcos River, remain unspoiled, and its business community continues to draw new markets to this region. Academically, from pre-kindergarden through high school and colleges, Seguin students continue, in greater numbers than ever, to distinguish themselves and their community. Since locating here in 1912, Texas Lutheran University has not only become a nationally ranked academic university, but is also a great part of Seguin's cultural heritage, with its many programs open and free to the public as well as being a cosponsor of the Mid-Texas Symphony. The Seguin Independent School District received the highest recognition by the state in 2009, being a "recognized" institution.

Churches abound. To drive through town or out in the county on a Sunday morning is to drive along quiet streets and roads. In town everyone knows that Wednesday night is not the best time to plan community meetings that may involve students because that is church night. But that does not mean Seguin does not know how to have a good time. Indeed, it is a drawing venue for many activities throughout the year from across the state.

This then is a story of Seguin and Guadalupe County's religious and educational development that began almost as soon as Seguin was founded. It is a touching story in many respects because it is a continuum of what was, what is today, and what will be to come.

The first organizational meeting for formal education was in 1846, although churches up to then had provided school instruction. By 1850, two schools were built. One was Guadalupe High School, which was one-half male academy and one-half female academy, each having its own separate location in the school building.

The second school, also built in 1850 by the inventor of Parks Concrete, Dr. John Parks, is today known as St. James Catholic School. Originally it was St. Joseph's Academy. Today St. James enjoys the distinction of being the oldest continuously used schoolhouse in the state of Texas.

Perhaps one of the most memorable schools is the structure now called the Mary B. Erskine School, or "Mary B," named after its early and famous teacher Mary Brown Erskine. Originally the school was Seguin High School even though the elementary students were on the first floor and the high school students were on the second floor.

The May Fete was one of the highlights of the academic year at the Mary B. Erskine School. This 1925 photograph shows how extensive and festive the students dressed for the queen's court. During these early-20th-century years, many students walked to school, sometimes over many miles. This was also true for the rural schools.

At one time, Kingsbury's population was greater than Seguin's. This was especially so during the oil boom of the late 1920s through the 1940s. This photograph included Frank "Doc" Schmidt in the buggy on the right. The school is just behind the young students. Today there are no schools in Kingsbury.

The original school for young African American students in Seguin was the Abraham Lincoln School. Eventually it was renamed Ball School in honor of William Baton Ball, a prominent black educator. The original structure was one story, but as the black population increased, a two-story school building was constructed, as seen in this photograph. The high school's name was Ball High School, an extension of Ball School.

One of the highlights of the year for Ball High School students was homecoming. In this 1951 photograph is Ball's queen and homecoming court, all gathered in the gym. Ball High School developed a strong reputation and following in its band activities. Under the direction of coach Leslie "Goldie" Harris, many young men and women learned lifelong values in all the sports.

This is the last graduating class from the new Ball High School, relocated to 620 Krezdorn Street. In the first row, second from left, is Fred Wilson, and in the second row, just behind him, is Morris Brothers. H. F. Wilson was principal, and upon integration in 1966, he became Seguin High School's first black assistant principal.

There were a number of county schools in rural areas. Many of them are shown in this chapter, such as Guadalupe Valley School. In this 1917 photograph, the students were well dressed; all the boys even had on shoes. In many rural communities, depending on weather conditions, times were either good, bad, or in between, and money for clothing was hard to come by.

In later years, as seen in this 1935 photograph, the Guadalupe Valley School became the McQueeney School. It appears these elementary students were celebrating May Fete perhaps just outside the school. Although many students looked forward to the end of the school year, they also knew there was work waiting for them on their farms.

In the northeastern part of the county was the Weinert School, located in the Weinert community. This is the only known photograph of the school, taken before 1910. It is believed the teacher was Lizzie Maddox, and indeed, she had her hands full with this widely spaced age group. Today neither the Weinert community nor the school remains as such.

The O'Daniel community is located toward the southwest part of Guadalupe County. Sandy Elm School was built in 1914. Its upstairs was used by the Woodmen of the World lodge. The chimney was in the center of the building, and the front entrance porch was the stage. Edna B. Herbold was the teacher.

This 1925 photograph of Laubach School shows some barefoot youngsters. The school was located in a comfortable area near the Geronimo Creek. The Laubach community also had a *sangerhalle* (singing hall) and bowling alley. Laubach remains a viable community to this day just north and east of Seguin. The school was later renamed the San Geronimo School.

The Sweet Home area is south of Seguin and remains an active community. The Sweet Home School was one of six Rosenwald Foundation schools for black education in Guadalupe County that were funded in part by Sears and Roebuck president Julius Rosenwald in joint coordination with George Washington Carver to provide increased vocational education for students. The Sweet Home School is on the National Register of Historic Places.

One of the points the photographer was making about the Jahns School was that city schools had nothing on the country schools. The Jahns School was believed to be the first school with a bus to pick up the youngsters and safely return them home. They would have fit well with today's "destination imagination" youngsters, who are part of highly creative teams that compete both locally and nationwide. (Courtesy of Jody Dixon.)

Dowdy High School was located east of Seguin in the Darst Oil Field. The school was very strong in athletics, boasting a six-man football squad and a basketball team. The girls' sports program was excellent and won a number of regional tournaments. It is not uncommon to this day to hear their stories and enjoy their reunions.

Leissner School was west of Seguin going toward the New Berlin community. Pictured here is the school orchestra. From left to right are (seated) Gene Naumann, coronet; Myrtle Behrendt, organ; and Hubert Woerndel, coronet; (standing) Nola Behrendt, Willie Schulze, Fred Mueller, and Daniel Muehl, violin. Although the school no longer exists, Leissner School Road does.

The Navarro Schoolhouse still stands between Seguin and Geronimo, thanks to the preservation efforts of the Texas Agriculture Education and Heritage Center and Wilford Bartoskewitz. The school was named after Jose Antonio Navarro, who was one of three Hispanics to sign the Declaration of Independence. Through the original preservation efforts of Carolyn Bading, the school was restored and recently donated to the heritage center.

The Barbarossa School was only for Mexican Americans in the northern part of Guadalupe County in the Barbarossa community. The school no longer stands, but the community remains vibrant to this day and fosters its strong rural heritage. Elia J. Martinez was the teacher. Today nine-pin bowling is still played, and shuffleboard is available for contestants in the saloon.

The Tiemann School was located about 6 miles east of Seguin. This 1904 photograph shows E. W. Bartholomae, the teacher, in the center in the second row. Many of the area's descendants remember six-month school terms and much time spent hoeing and picking cotton on the blackland prairies of this region.

Sue Smith was the teacher in 1904 at the Cordova School in central Guadalupe County. She eventually moved to Seguin, where she was so respected that the Sue Smith School on Jefferson Street was named for her. She had a remarkable degree of patience and understanding for her many students.

Stories abound of the competitions between Elm Creek School in the western part of Guadalupe County and its eastern Guadalupe County rivals. Darst High School was often a powerhouse, and when Elm Creek beat Darst there was a sweet feeling for the Elm Creek athletes. On the other hand, there was always the "wait 'til next year" spirit in each of the schools.

Four well-dressed gentlemen in a pre-1920s roadster are passing in front of Lutheran College's first building, Old Main. Lutheran College relocated from Brenham to Seguin in 1912, and its doors have remained open ever since. Although Old Main is no longer there, its bell is preserved and rings at special events, such as homecoming and graduation, to this day.

As there were schools in early Seguin and Guadalupe County, so too were there churches, often patterned after their sister parishes, such as the Methodist Episcopal Church South, seen here. Pictured from left to right are the confirmation class of Annette Gombert, Irma Petry, a Reverend Koch (pastor), Lilly Gerdes, and Edward Woehler. Halm Portrait Studio in Seguin, which preceded the Weiss Studio, took the picture.

Also in the Elm Creek community was Christ Lutheran Church. This 1961 photograph by the Leon Studio included a frontal shot of the narthex with steeple. Christ Lutheran Church has been recognized by the State of Texas with a Texas State Historical Marker. Today the church remains vibrant as its history continues to grow.

The Redeemer Church in Zuehl, located in the western part of Guadalupe County, was dedicated on October 14, 1900, on Gin Road. By 1950, it had become affiliated with the United Church of Christ. The Zuehl community continues to be a leading agricultural sector in Guadalupe County as it journeys into the 21st century.

This stately rural church is the St. John Lutheran Church in Marion, about 12 miles west-northwest of Seguin. It was built in 1923 and is located at the corner of Cunningham and San Antonio Streets. This photograph was taken in 1964, and the new church was built in 1967.

The Lutheran church (American Lutheran Church [ALC]) was located at the Weinert School and was founded by a Pastor Webber, pictured below in the second row, far right. From left to right are (first row) Raymond Erxleben, Leland Lorenz, Alvin Hagemann, Nelson Erxleben, Leroy Lorenz, Carlene Wright, and Jeannette Stautzenberger. This photograph was taken about 1939 or 1940. (Courtesy of Raymond Erxelben.)

Friedens Church, or *Kirche*, began in the Frankfort School at a founders' meeting on January 18, 1896. By the late summer of 1904, the cornerstone was laid for the German Lutheran church at Lone Oak, 8 miles north of Geronimo. Today more than 100 years of services have been held at Friedens Church, which is now associated with the United Church of Christ.

The rural Sweet Home community was not only fortunate to enjoy a strong school system supported by the Rosenwald Foundation, but was also fortunate to have a strong Baptist congregation. This is well evidenced by the size of its 1954 congregation in celebration of one of its anniversaries. Although the congregation is smaller today, its spirit is as vibrant as in yesteryear.

The churches in Seguin were also binding pillars of the community. This German Methodist church was established in 1874 toward the end of the Civil War Reconstruction era. It was built on East Gonzales Street where present-day La Trinidad Methodist Church is located. The Reverend E. C. Draeger was pastor when the church was built. His grandchildren included Eleanor Draeger, Viola Baker, Ruth Schuessler, and Dorothy Ryan.

Emanuel Lutheran Church was first established in 1870 on North Camp Street. Although the original structure no longer stands, the church remains at the same location. Like many of the Protestant churches built during that era, there is a single gabled roof with an inviting entrance into its narthex. Notice the elaborate fence with the arch at its entrance. Emanuel's service continues well into the 21st century.

The First United Methodist Church, when combined with the German Methodist congregations, was first located not too far from the original German Methodist church. This church was built on the corner of Mountain and River Streets until a newer structure was constructed on North Austin Street. Its architecture introduced a departure from the earlier churches by creating a more imposing building and adding some Gothic features.

Originally the Episcopal and Methodist churches in Seguin were known as the First Church or Methodist-Episcopal Church. The original church was established in 1853 and was located on South Austin Street. Today it has been moved and restored by the Seguin Conservation Society and is located on East Live Oak Street. This photograph shows the original St. Andrews Episcopal Church, built in 1876.

The Trinidad Methodist Church is now at the location of the original German Methodist church on East Gonzales Street. This 1965 photograph shows the dedication of the new wing, which is the sanctuary. Today the Trinidad Methodist Church is a vibrant participant in Seguin's church community and enjoys playing host to a number of activities throughout the year.

St. James-Field Mass and Bazaar

St. James Catholic Church on South Camp Street celebrated Seguin's 1838 centennial birthday with a field Mass and bazaar on April 24, 1938. It was held on the grounds of the convent and school, the oldest continuously used school in Texas. Part of the rectory can be seen to the right. Next to it is the church.

Wesley Harper United Methodist Church (UMC) celebrated its 132nd anniversary in 2010. Wesley Chapel United Protestant Methodist Church was organized in 1887. The 1919 Mill Creek Church was organized east of Seguin and merged with Harper Chapel, named after Maggie Harper. The present-day Wesley Harper UMC was established in 1970.

On December 12, 1908, Our Lady of Guadalupe Church was dedicated on Jones Street by Bishop John A. Forest. Across the street was its schoolhouse, served by the Sisters of Charity. Their convent, a two-story structure, was just one block away. The church has continued to serve the Mexican American Catholics of Seguin and Guadalupe County for more than 100 years. Today it is located on West Krezdorn and North Guadalupe Streets.

Five

A CROSSROADS
OF COMMERCE
1940s–1980s

Although this chapter focuses on the 1940s to the 1980s, there are also photographs that will appear serving the transitional years prior to the 1940s and after the 1980s. This is not done to confuse the reader but to serve as a bridge between those events already presented in this book and those that have yet to be presented.

Within Seguin, Guadalupe County, and south-central Texas, this period of pre–World War II to the beginning of the end of the cold war was an era that framed and marked the community's modern personality, which continues to evolve through its journey into the 21st century.

In 1938, Seguin celebrated its first 100 years as a town and then a city. Guadalupe County, for all practical purposes, was also 100 years old but officially could not make this claim until 1986 due to its not being officially recognized as a county until 1846. Regardless, the history of Seguin and Guadalupe County are so interrelated even to this day that one cannot be excluded from the other.

In 1940, Seguin's economy had not changed dramatically from its agricultural antecedents. Farming, ranching, and agricultural support agencies continued to dominate the economy, while the people and their collective personalities defined a rural way of life. There were no stoplights in downtown Seguin, just blinking lights at Court and Austin Streets and Court and River Streets. U.S. Highway 90 was Seguin's first outer loop. Within the city limits, it is called Kingsbury Street. U.S. Highway 90A forks off U.S. Highway 90 as it enters Seguin from San Antonio and continues through downtown and leaves to the east going through Gonzales and beyond.

During this time, Seguin's transportation infrastructure also changed from north to south with State Highway 123 becoming Seguin's most recent outer loop, as it spread southward toward neighboring Stockdale and Karnes City, intersecting with U.S. Highways 90 and 90A. This period of the 1940s through the 1980s was a defining era for Seguin's future as it inched toward the 21st century.

Of the many rural communities that comprised Guadalupe County, these are the only ones left. Gone are the days of such communities as Weinert, Galle, Randolph, and many more. Regardless of urban encroachment from surrounding counties, Guadalupe County has enjoyed maintaining and nurturing its agricultural heritage. (Courtesy of Stanley Naumann.)

Darst Oil Field had its competition not only in neighboring counties, but also within Guadalupe County. North and east of the Darst Oil Field was the Gander Slough community that was a part of the Luling Oil Field. This photograph shows Gander Slough's Main Street, a muddy thoroughfare, and the OK Café. Gander Slough was known as a "tough place."

As Seguin's men and women were going off to World War II, Guadalupe County's extensive farming base became critical to food production for America's troops. Mexico provided thousands of immigrants to work the fields of the southwest and midwestern states. Seen here on West Kingsbury Street are immigrants shucking corn.

Capt. Alvin Mueller was one of Seguin's most decorated heroes during World War II. He was awarded the Distinguished Flying Cross and survived the Japanese attack on Clark Air Field in the Philippines at the same time Hawaii and Pearl Harbor were being attacked. He received a hero's homecoming at the train depot.

The Harris Café was a popular gathering place on downtown Austin Street. Mrs. E. L. Harris, pictured, was Bill Huffmann's grandmother. Harris was known throughout Seguin for helping families who ran out of food ration stamps during World War II. She made sure no one went hungry and provided meals when needed.

Seguin has always had some form of entertainment for the public, whether it was the community band at the bandstand (gazebo), opera houses, or a spontaneous parade. The first movie theater was the Wonderland Theater, owned by J. D. Petty, which was located on the east side of the 100 block of North Austin Street. It was a favorite venue for youngsters who were thrilled by the early silent movies. Replacing the Wonderland Theater were the 1938 Palace Theater and, later, the Texas Theater.

The Palace Theater was popular under H. A. Daniels and continues to serve the community under the direction of Danny Daniels. It was famous for the many movie stars who came to Seguin, such as John Wayne. Today the Palace Theater is a popular venue for special events, such as the Seguin Theater performers, local musicians, and special movie events.

Willy Weiss, who emigrated from Germany and settled in New Braunfels, founded the Weiss Studio. He hired Nelda Germann and Leon Kubala while they were still in high school. In 1944 or 1945, he sold the studio to them after they married. The Leon Studio prospered until it closed in the early 21st century. From left to right are Weiss, Kubala, and Henrietta Weiss in the original studio on North Austin Street.

This 1945 photograph of Juan Seguin Elementary School students reflects their interest in music. This is their rhythm band, complete with musical instruments and singers. The school initially served the Hispanic students in Seguin. However, because of a lack of space for all Hispanic students at Juan Seguin, a number attended other schools in the city. The school enjoys a prominent place in the Hispanic history of Seguin.

The original high school in Seguin was known as Seguin High School, a two-story structure with a basement. The high school students were taught on the second floor, and the elementary students were on the first floor. The building burned down but was replaced with a new one. Later it was renamed the Mary B. Erskine Elementary School in honor of the former teacher (shown in the portrait). Honoring Erskine are (from left to right) principal Clarence Little, Maude Erskine Baer, Libby Erskine Holloman, and parent-teacher association president Pat Liberty.

Standing from left to right are Robert Zoboroski (Seguin Police Department), Bill Whitworth, Melvin Harborth (county sheriff), Bill Haiyasoso, and Bill Gillian of the Texas Department of Public Safety. They are watching county judge Jim Sagebiel and Seguin's first woman mayor, Betty Jean Jones, sign a proclamation for a national police memorial honoring officers killed on duty.

Although Pres. Harry S. Truman did not integrate the armed forces until the Korean War, African Americans proudly fought on the frontier and in both world wars. They formed their own American Legion in Seguin, as seen in this 1948 Leon Studio photograph. Although the men are not identified, their service to their country is not forgotten.

Starcke Park, the city's municipal park, was dedicated in 1938. In addition to its original nine-hole golf course, a large swimming pool was built that became a focal point of Seguin's life and pageantry well into the late 20th century. Beauty pageants, swim competitions, and animated voices floated across the Guadalupe River and the golf course.

In 1948, Marvin Selig founded SMI, a steel-making plant, on the property of Seguin's flour mill north and west of downtown. It has been a big supporter of many events, including its parade entries, as seen in this 1960 photograph. SMI continues today as CMC Steel-Texas and remains a strong supporter of Seguin.

Black Beauty, owned and trained by S. Ward, is seen winning its event on November 12, 1936, at the fairgrounds racetrack. Horses throughout Seguin and Guadalupe County's history have always been a point of pride and commerce. From horse racing to Teddy Roosevelt recruiting horses in Seguin for the Spanish-American War, Bobby Hawkin's national cutting horse championships, and today's many breeders and youngsters practicing their horsemanship, the horse legacy continues.

In the winter of 1942, chamber of commerce manager Garfield Kiel had the chamber sponsor a small parade. Leon Kubala's sisters Evelyn and Pearl (seated on top of the elephant) volunteered for the task, knowing they would be rewarded with a soda in Williams Drug Store, seen in the back of the photograph next to the second fire station.

R. A. Sanders has everyone's rapt attention as he shares ideas and suggestions with the ladies at the Negro Egg and Poultry Show in 1949. Young and old throughout the county were there and continue today to be ardent supporters of the fairs and livestock shows. Each October is fair month for Guadalupe County, and participation increases with each passing year.

Here are two well-known men in Guadalupe County during their days: Buck Bergfeld (left) was the city's marshal, while Phil Medlin (right) was a popular county sheriff in the 1950s and 1960s. Bergfeld always led the parades, and Medlin, with his horse deputy, often performed for schools, doing tricks. He was a noted singer and gave swimming lessons at the Starcke Park pool.

One of Guadalupe County's legendary fiddlers was J. "Box" Roberts. He lived in Kingsbury, but to him, the world was music. Pictured here from left to right are (sitting) Billy Mitchell and Dan Crieder; (standing) Roberts and Earl Seay (playing the banjo). Today one of Guadalupe County Fair's major events is the fiddlers contest for young and old. Not surprisingly, Roberts's descendents are some of the organizers of the competition.

Shelly Mayfield grew up in Seguin and graduated from Seguin High School. He went on to become an accomplished professional golfer and a club professional. In this photograph, Mayfield (left) beat Dr. Cary Middlecoff in the 1954 San Antonio Texas Open. Today he is in the Texas Professional Golfers Hall of Fame. He was personally nominated by all-time great Ben Hogan.

Legendary football coach Jim Wacker led the Texas Lutheran College Bulldogs to several national championships in their division in the early to mid-1970s. Pictured in this photograph is the 1973 squad. Many of his former players still reminisce about the values Wacker instilled in them. Wacker seemed to produce winning programs wherever he went.

In 1960, Seguin High School's baseball team won the state championship by defeating Kilgore by a score of 3-1 in the semifinals and Snyder in the finals by a score of 3-0. Baseball continues to be one of the most played sports in Seguin and Guadalupe County. From left to right are (first row) manager Larry Swisher, manager Buddy Stewart, and manager Alvin Siltman; (second row) Jim Langley, Jimmy Luns, Mat Pogar, Fred Fuentes, Yankee Camarillo, Freddy Torres, Abel Solis, Charles Hartenstein, Charles Gregg, Robert Kramer, and Arlon Kichner; (third row) coach Raymond Erxleben, Gilbert Huth, K. Wesley Doerr, Johnny Zunker, Harvey Kutac, Jeep Kiel, Joel Tigett, John Hoermnn, and coach Bill McElduff.

Future champions in many Seguin sports are seen coming up the ranks as viewed in this photograph of R. A. Saunders (standing, far left). Many members of his 1954 Guadalupe County 4-H club went on to win honors under all-time coaching great Leslie "Goldie" Harris at Ball High School. Between Saunders and Harris, youngsters learned many lifelong skills.

Hollywood comedian Joe E. Brown loved baseball. Thanks to H. A. Daniels and the Palace Theater, Brown visited the fairgrounds baseball diamond to throw a few balls. Needless to say, that game was well attended and appreciated by fans and players alike in the late 1950s. Daniels also brought many other famous Hollywood personalities to Seguin, including John Wayne.

Ramón Salazar Sr. opened Salazar's Grocery Store in 1954 at 702 Newton Street. Pictured is Salazar standing in his well-stocked grocery, which sold traditional items, including many of the foods cherished in the Hispanic community. His son Ramón Salazar Jr. continued the store's operations in 1962 and sold it in 2002. (Courtesy of Ramón Salazar.)

Although Pres. Dwight D. Eisenhower was unable to campaign in Seguin, his popular wife, Mamie, made a stop at the Seguin train depot in 1950. She was presented with a bouquet of roses and the applause of her and the president's admirers. Other famous politicians and family members visiting Seguin included senator and later president Lyndon B. Johnson. His wife, Lady Bird Johnson, also visited Seguin.

Numerous Seguin and Guadalupe County citizens have held elected political posts at the state and national level, including H. F. Weinert, John Ireland, Harry Wurzbach, Charles H. Donegan, and Edmund Kuempel. At the state level, it was John Traeger (pictured at left) who diligently served in the House of Representatives and the senate for a combined 24 years, helping shepherd many beneficial programs for Texas.

The seven Timmermann sisters of Geronimo appeared on national and regional radio, as well as on the major television networks. Pictured in this 1955 photograph from left to right are (first row) Melitta, Wanda, Meta, and Hilda; (second row) Tekla, Stella, and Willie Mae. They are in front of a stained-glass window of First Protestant Church in New Braunfels. Their great-grandfather Rev. Louis Cachaund-Ervendberg helped establish the church in 1846.

Six

Twenty-first Century Metamorphosis
1990s–2010

In a sense, this chapter is a denouement of sorts. The photographs capture modern-day Seguin from the 1970s and 1980s through the present. The reader will still sense the agricultural and manufacturing heritage of this region but will also understand that the future is Seguin and Guadalupe County's to determine. Many of the photographs in this chapter depict the younger generation being guided by the older generation. It is this spirit of continuity that the founders envisioned and that their subsequent generations have fostered.

To be sure, there have been failures in the economy, recessions, natural and man-made disasters, and family tragedies, but the successes have far outweighed these detours of life. This is evidenced by the photographs depicting parades, Future Farmers of America, scouting programs, and leading women who continue to affect the community through their civic stewardship, the preservation of history and the building of the new, and planning and quietly developing the infrastructure that will nourish growth in a positive way.

Thus what is shared in this chapter can be viewed as a community's continuation of life rather than the life cycle of a community. Vibrancy, hard work, a blending of local government working with community participation, and planning and execution constantly draw businesses, churches, and educational opportunities into Seguin, its county, and its region.

The Starcke Park swimming pool not only had swimming and diving contests and beauty pageants, but also swimming lessons and youth activities. Seen here is a group of young ladies waiting to be judged in a bathing suit competition during a warm summer's evening pool program. These venues attracted large audiences.

H. A. "Lefty" Stackhouse was not only a well-known local golfer on the PGA tour, but also the head professional at the Starcke Park golf course. For many years, he had his own driving range on the east side. He is shown here with his wife, Evelyn. During his many years at the golf course, he saw Seguin High School golfers win four consecutive class 3-A state championships.

A number of women have played major roles in Seguin's development. One such lady was Louella Huffmann Brown. Her vision was that of Seguin's health care system being taken to a higher level in the 1960s. Through her efforts, a state-of-the-art hospital was built on East Court Street, and the Weinert Street hospital eventually became a governmental office subsidiary.

Another leading lady was Leonie Pape, an accomplished pianist and teacher. Many of her students won top honors in competitions and recitals throughout the region and state. Her gifts became the gifts of her students, and many took their skills with them as they played in not only the junior high and senior high school bands, but some formed their own bands.

The Broken Hearts Band was one of a number of popular groups that emerged in the 1960s. Pictured here are, from left to right, Frutoso "Fruit" Balderas (drums), Gilbert Gonzales (saxophone), Raymond Salazar (guitar), Bobby Gonzales (singer), Rudy Machado (keyboard), Jimmy Solis (saxophone), Jesse Carrillo (saxophone), and George Soto (guitar). The Broken Hearts were inducted into the Tejano Music Hall of Fame on February 1, 1992. (Courtesy of Ramón Salazar.)

Another well-known musical group in Seguin was the Turbans, led by Doug Parker. From left to right are Al Belmarez, Chester McIntyre, Walter Friedeck, Parker, and Charles McIntyre. The Turbans played a variety of tunes and were often called upon to play at local dances. (Courtesy of Doug Parker.)

Each Christmas, the Timmermann sisters opened their house to the public to see their tree and re-creations of their great-grandfather's orphanage under the tree. Louis C. Ervendberg, the first pastor for the German immigrants in New Braunfels, started the orphanage near Gruene, which remains occupied to this day. This re-created orphanage scene is currently on display with the Bob Bullock Museum in Austin.

Austin Street is alive with young and old alike during the Christmas parade. Entries of all types reflect this spirit and receive loud, heartfelt applause as they pass by the onlookers and the reviewing stand at Austin and Court Streets. Children have always been a major part of Seguin's many parades. If their parents are not sponsors on the floats, then someone who is known to the family is.

Another part of the Christmas festivities is Las Posadas. Locally it began at Our Lady of Guadalupe Catholic Church in the Hispanic community. Today it is an interdenominational event that begins at city hall on North Austin Street with Mary and Joseph leading the participants as they seek lodging at various buildings for the birthing of Mary's child. (Courtesy of Stanley Naumann.)

Many communities have Fourth of July parades. In large cities, there may be any number of suburban parades. Seguin has had such a parade for about 100 years and proudly calls it the "Biggest Small 4th of July Parade in Texas." The earliest parades were led by the fire department. Today they fall under the leadership of Main Street director Mary Jo Filip.

Seguin's parades enjoy many entries that represent myriad businesses and groups throughout the county and invited guests from other cities. Such is reflected in this photograph, featuring young *charreadas* on their splendidly groomed horses. These *charreadas* came from the San Antonio Charro Association, which performs throughout this region.

No parade would be complete without Don Richey dressed as a jovial Uncle Sam atop his late-19th-century-styled bicycle. Richey has been a feature of Seguin's parades for many years. It almost seems that a Fourth of July parade without his presence would be incomplete.

In the 2004 Fourth of July parade, the community wanted to openly honor its heroes. As a result, the men and women who have served in Iraq and Afghanistan were honored as the grand marshals for the parade. Seguin and Guadalupe County have always honored their veterans since their founding. (Courtesy of Stanley Naumann.)

Each October, in conjunction with the annual three-day Pecan Festival that attracts visitors from across the state, many activities, including the hanging of the wreath at the base of the Juan Seguin statue in the city park, occur. Another is the popular Hats Off to Juan Seguin contest, held outside the historic Oak Tavern. Needless to say, the judges are challenged. (Courtesy of Stanley Naumann.)

Also held each October at the coliseum and fairgrounds, now the Seguin Event Center, is a two-day, two-night event called Buck Fever. This popular outdoorsman-hunter-fisherman event has hundreds of booths from local vendors and from across the state. There are events for judging trophy deer, to fishing for children, rock climbing, and archery contests. Thousands flock to this popular event each fall. (Courtesy of Stanley Naumann.)

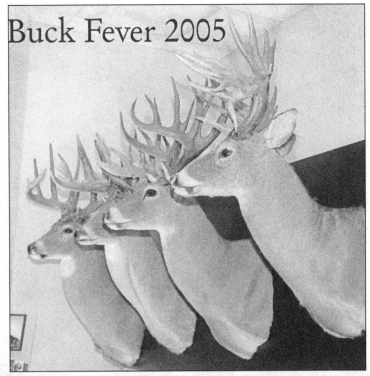

Buck Fever 2005

On the northwest side of the county courthouse is a small section beautifully sculpted by James Dethredge, owner of Carter Memorials. This landscaped garden is in honor of veterans from all wars. Not only are there engraved bricks with the names of those who have served, but also a lighted memorial wall and benches. Former mayor Ed Gotthardt and Basil Karms spearheaded this project. (Courtesy of Stanley Naumann.)

Scouting today is as cherished as it was in the early 20th century. In this homemade father-and-son car race were Cub Scout Pack 107. From left to right in pairs are first-place winners Karl Marvin Krueger and his son Karl, runners-up Eddie Morales Jr. and his son Eddie Jr., and the third-place finishers Arlyn Hartfiel and his son Michael Hartfiel.

Brian Naumann, second from left, is receiving Boy Scout's highest achievement, the Order of the Arrow. Standing to his left is Ed Moss and to his right are Ruben Rodriguez and Bob Magins. Naumann represents the dedication and determination that is needed to receive this award. The Cub Scout, Boy Scout, and Explorer programs continue well into the 21st century in Seguin.

Dr. Clarence B. Friday was Seguin's first African American physician. His first baby delivery was Coleta Byrd on the day after his arrival. Friday's office was on the 100 block of North Crockett and Court Streets. At one point in his distinguished career, he held positions in the African American Medical Association. He is pictured with his daughter Dorothy (sitting) and wife, Leila (standing).

Celebrating the 75th anniversary of the Girl Scouts of America by releasing balloons at the central park's fountain are Brownies, Girl Scouts, their adult leaders, and family members. They joined all their fellow troops nationwide to celebrate this significant event. Today Seguin's Girl Scouts remain as popular as ever and continue to contribute to the city's healthy sense of community participation.

There are numerous homes throughout the Seguin and Guadalupe County area that have been recognized as Texas historical sites entered on the National Register of Historic Places. One example is the Joseph Sonka home, built by Joseph Sonka between 1881 and 1883 of bricks from his nearby brickyard. It served as a hospital from 1913 to 1915 and has been continuously occupied to this date.

The 1940s Los Aztecas baseball team was one of several Hispanic baseball teams in Seguin. Another was the Los Mambos team. The competition was keen between all of Seguin's teams, just as they are today. All of Seguin's semiprofessional baseball teams were a big draw for the public. Out of these contests arose the current Smokey Joe Williams Baseball Field at the fairgrounds, where so many games are played.

One of the many celebrations held at Sebastopol each year is the Abashai Mercer Dickson chapter of the Daughters of the Republic of Texas's March 2 Toast to Texas in honor of Texas's declaration of independence from Mexico. Students from surroundings schools participate in this event. Numerous state and local officials and leaders of many civic groups also participate or attend.

In the Seguin Conservation Society's Heritage Village are a number of pioneer structures. Two of them are the Los Nogales building and the Dietz Doll House. The Los Nogales structure was built sometime before the 1836 Texas Revolution and was said to have been Seguin's first post office. Louis Dietz, a German immigrant, built the dollhouse for his daughter and originally attached it to the entrance of their house.

Seguin's present-day city hall was built about the same time as the new, or fourth, courthouse. It is located on the 200 block of North River Street and East Gonzales Street, one block north of the courthouse. Thus far, it continues to house the entire municipal government offices and is easily accessible to the public. It was built on the site of the former Dibrell house.

Perhaps one of the most uniquely designed structures in Seguin's downtown commercial district is the Donegan building, which once was Seguin Savings and Loan. Today it houses the Seguin Area Chamber of Commerce. Its 1960s architecture makes it an eye-catcher. Little known by many is that the basement serves as a nuclear fallout shelter, complete with rooms (now offices) and separate shower-toilet facilities for men and women.

As land disappears to urban and industrial development, the spirit of agriculture is kept alive throughout each of the school districts in Seguin in Guadalupe County, Navarro (in Geronimo), Marion, and Schertz-Cibolo (in Cibolo). This youngster shows that the spirit of cowboys, rodeos, and pure grit have a good future.

These Future Farmers of America at Navarro High School proudly display their winnings at their district and area levels of competition. From left to right are (first row) Bryan Ivey, Alicia Orme, Lucy Boelterm, and Ashley Miklas; (second row) Sharee Robinson, Heather Fiscus, Shanda Elley, and Hayden James. Not pictured is Monica Mueck.

Perhaps one of the best-known restaurants was the Silver Dollar, located on West U.S. Highway 90. Its story reflects the era of Seguin when there was gambling in the basement from the 1940s through the 1960s to becoming El Ranchito. Today the building is occupied by the Woodmen of the World.

Seven

A Legacy from the Past
Today and Tomorrow

In this final chapter, the past 172 years of Seguin's history reflect its effect on the present. Seguin is no longer a rural community, although parts of Guadalupe County remain rural to this day. But with increasing population shifts, more roads, and increased commerce, the truly rural part of this region's history is changing.

What is not changing is the vitality of life from every corner of Seguin and Guadalupe County. Mom-and-pop stores still continue regardless of the successes of the major chain stores that have been accepted by the community. Education continues to enjoy a high priority in each of Guadalupe County's communities. Agriculture is flourishing, except during the infamous 2007–2009 central Texas droughts. Manufacturers listed on the New York Stock Exchange have their businesses in Seguin and Guadalupe County, including Alamo Group, Caterpillar, Continental, CMC Steel-Texas, Hexcel, MiniGrip, and Tyson Foods.

Culture and celebrations continue today in their own forms, as seen through the Mid-Texas Symphony, Teatro De Artes de Juan Seguin, the Oakwood Art League, the parades, and certainly recreational water sports along the graceful Guadalupe River for all ages of boys, girls, men, women, and clubs. And for special interest activities, the Federated Women's Club remains vital to the community, as do the Seguin Conservation Society, Rotary Club, Kiwanis Club, Lion's Club, Habitat for Humanity, the Christian Cupboard, and all the church activities that abound throughout Seguin and Guadalupe County.

It all started in 1838 along the springs of Walnut Creek with 44 investors. Their vision became today's vitality and reality. The future remains as exciting and unknown as it did then. Seguin's continuing journey surely will be as palpable as its past.

As can be seen on this monument dedicated to the German Immigrant Trail by the Guadalupe-Blanco River Authority, in the 1840s and 1850s, Seguin was an integral part of that trail from Indianola to the gateway and the Hill Country in New Braunfels. The monument is in the central city park. Many descendents of these early and tenacious immigrants remain in this area today.

In 1838, Seguin celebrated its 100th anniversary with celebrations throughout the community. There was a new county courthouse, and the Max Starcke Park was opened with a golf course and swimming pool, along with other events. In 2013, Seguin will be 175 years old with a bright future ahead. This monument is also in Seguin's central square (park).

Today Seguin still recognizes its leaders and community contributors. City park, or the original city square, is still the focus of such celebrations. Melvin Voight was the 2008 Down Towner of the Year in Seguin's historical Main Street district. Voight is the proprietor of the ever-popular historic Oak Tavern on East Gonzales Street. (Courtesy of Stanley Naumann.)

One of Seguin's most popular minstrel groups is the Harleys. The Harleys, founded by Pastor Greg Ronning of Texas Lutheran University, plays 1950s, 1960s, and contemporary music for fund-raisers for not-for-profit organizations. This fun-loving community-spirited group is seen below being recognized as 2008 volunteers in Seguin by the city. From left to right are Mike McGrew, Greg Ronning, and Dr. John Masterson. (Courtesy of Stanley Naumann.)

KWED radio station, 1580 AM, was founded in 1947 and became known as the voice of Seguin. Garfield Kiel was the first general manager. Early announcers were Ellie Selig, Faye Chessher, and Stan McKenzie. Pictured from left to right are (seated) Rosie Ornelas, Edith Kiel, and Stan McKenzie; (standing) G. P. Kiel, Sharon Kiel Wollack, and Ken Kiel. (Courtesy of Stanley Naumann.)

Starcke Furniture's beginning was in 1908 when Hilmar Starcke became a business partner with Mrs. F. Weisskopff and her husband's Economy Furniture on North Austin Street. Starcke bought the store in 1910 and moved it to its present location in 1912. The store was built by architect Atlee Ayers on behalf of Edgar Nolte. Pictured are Frank Starcke (left) and Hilmar Starcke, descendents of Nolte. (Courtesy of Stanley Naumann.)

The Texas Agricultural Education and Heritage Center was founded by longtime farmers and ranchers Wilford and Betty Bartoskewitz in 2003. They felt that through offering hands-on experiences with the agricultural industry, such knowledge would touch many of tomorrow's lives. Cutting the ribbon are the directors (from left to right) Mel Grones, unidentified, Kermit Westerholm, Robert Raetzsch, Wilford and Betty Bartoskowitz, Gene Dietert, Ron Heinemeyer, and Seguin mayor Betty Ann Matthies. (Courtesy of Stanley Naumann.)

Not often does anyone discover a site once built and operated on the backs of slaves, but local former archaeological steward Richard Kinz did. Soon slave descendents began to visit the site in Guadalupe County. Not long afterward, the Wilson family established its foundation and soon will open its Wilson Pottery Museum along Walnut Creek, not far from where Seguin was founded. (Courtesy of Stanley Naumann.)

Throughout its history, Seguin has given birth to local banks, such as Nolte Bank, Citizens State Bank, and Seguin State Bank, just to name a few. As happens with progress and expansion, these banks were absorbed by regional and national banks. Today only one locally founded and owned bank remains—First Commercial Bank, with Mark Williams as a leading founder and chairman of the board of directors. (Courtesy of Stanley Naumann.)

Perhaps one of the most dramatic fires happened in 2001. The 1869 Vivroux Hardware Store burned and was gutted, and the fire raged all night. Gene Vivroux, a direct family descendant and the owner, restored as much as he could. Today one part is an antique store, and the other is the Chiro Java Wi-Fi café. (Courtesy of Danny Daniels.)

Business continues well into the 21st century, as evidenced by the spirit shown at the 2009 Seguin Area's Chamber of Commerce Business Showcase. The staff of the *Seguin-Gazette Enterprise* newspaper won this year's best-decorated booth in the city coliseum. From left to right are chamber of commerce ambassador Fanny Harkins, Becca Polanco, Kristi Ranft, Pat Castillo (holding the plaque), Gayelynn Olsovski, and publisher Neice Bell. (Courtesy of Stanley Naumann.)

Barbeque is a passion in the Seguin region. Local native Chris Elley won the South by Southwest best short film on Texas barbeque. Many excellent barbeque places are in Seguin, such as Davila's Bar-B-Q, owned by Edward Davila and founded by his father, Raul, in 1957. The Davilas moved to Seguin in 1959. In 1973and 1974, they bought King Bee's, where they remain today. (Courtesy of Stanley Naumann.)

One of Seguin's care-taking mainstays has historically been Madam Sophie's Palm Reading service for many questions and concerns in people's personal lives. Located on East Court Street, Madam Sophie's is in one of the few remaining houses that existed when Texas Lutheran University (then Lutheran College) relocated to Seguin in 1912. (Courtesy of Stanley Naumann.)

Neighborhood barbershops remain in Seguin. One such barbershop is McKnight's on North Saunders Street. It is an inviting location for Seguin's African American community, where traditional hairstyles can be maintained and friendly conversations are ongoing at the same time with the barber and those waiting their turns. Traditions such as these help keep and maintain Seguin's friendliness. (Courtesy of Stanley Naumann.)

One of the historically longtime Mexican food restaurants is El Ranchito. Founded 70 years ago by Juanita Cardenas in 1945, the first restaurant was on 607 West Kingsbury Street. Since that time, it has been family run and operated, and has grown in its service to the community. After moving to the Silver Dollar on West Kingsbury Street from 1967 to 1996, it is now located on North Highway 123. (Courtesy of Stanley Naumann.)

What would a modern community be without a snow cone place? JoAnn and Stanley Naumann converted an old house on South Austin Street near the coliseum and Starcke Park into such an island of respite for young and old from the south-central Texas sweltering heat. Shaded by native live oaks with picnic tables, it is an outdoor oasis. It serves more than 100 different varieties. (Courtesy of Stanley Naumann.)

An enduring downtown mom-and-pop store is City Cleaners, owned and operated by the Luis Rodriguez family. It was bought in 1970 from the Buerger family. It maintains its simple ways, including no air-conditioning, hard workers in the cleaning and pressing room, and a foot-pump sewing machine. (Courtesy of Stanley Naumann.)

The 2009 Toast to Texas was a huge success at the Sebastopol House State Park. Podium guests from left to right are a Mr. Zorn, Dr. Irene Garza (Seguin School District superintendent), Nora Naumann (Mercer Dickson chapter of the Daughters of the Republic of Texas), Dottsy Dwyer (Texas Country Music Hall of Fame), Mayor Betty Ann Matthies, and a buffalo soldier from the San Antonio chapter of the Buffalo Soldiers. (Courtesy of Stanley Naumann.)

Every spring under the guidance of Main Street director Mary Jo Filip, there is a Walnut Creek Cleanup Project. There are extensive plans that will eventually see Walnut Creek as a public linear parkway extending from near Texas Lutheran University through downtown to Starcke Park. Pictured from left to right are Trevor Anderson, Troy De Palermo, Colby De Palermo, Travis Anderson, and Taylor Anderson from Boy Scouts Troop 107. (Courtesy of Stanley Naumann.)

Within Guadalupe County, there are five high schools in four independent school districts (ISD): Seguin High School, Marion High School, Navarro High School, Steele High School, and Samuel Clemens High School in the Universal City-Schertz-Cibolo ISD. Pictured is the newest high school, the Byron P. Steele II High School, located in Cibolo. (Courtesy of Stanley Naumann.)

Seguin celebrated its first mural with its committee, comprised of (from left to right) Pat Schulze of the Seguin Oakwood Art League, Matt Chase, Nan Udell, Roger Betschler, and Main Street director Mary Jo Filip. The mural was placed on the south side of the historic Vivroux Hardware Store, now Chiro Java. The mural depicts the earliest settlers from all walks of life in early Seguin. (Courtesy of Stanley Naumann.)

At the January 31, 2009, ground-breaking for Caterpillar's new manufacturing plant is Terry Trevino. She is the director of the Seguin Economic Development Corporation in Seguin's municipal government, along with coworker Kate Silvas. They steadfastly and quietly acquired the land for Caterpillar, worked with state representative Edmund Kuempel, sought out Texas state incentives, and handled a myriad of tasks to complete the deal for Caterpillar. (Courtesy of Stanley Naumann.)

Pictured from left to right are unidentified, Senator Jeff Wentworth, Seguin's state representative Edmund Kuempel, and Peter Holt (out of frame). Holt is the chief executive officer of Caterpillar in San Antonio and owner of the five-time National Basketball Association champions San Antonio Spurs. Holt commented at the ground-breaking ceremony how quiet the whole transaction had been; even he was unaware of this project until 30 days prior to the event. (Courtesy of Stanley Naumann.)

Lt. Gov. David Dewhurst (left) and Gov. Rick Perry presented their thanks to Caterpillar and praised Seguin's ability to quietly work with municipalities, landowners, and many others in putting the Caterpillar package together. Seguin continues its history of private enterprises from mom-and-pop businesses to its large industries well into the 21st century. (Courtesy of Stanley Naumann.)

In 2006, the new bandstand in the city's central park was approved by the voters in a bond fund election. It was designed by architect Tim Aynesworth of Aynesworth Architect Consultants of Austin and was based upon historic photographs of the first bandstand. Local architect David Acterberg assisted in its historical interpretation. Once again the central square is a focus for all. (Courtesy of Stanley Naumann.)

Seguin's first hospital was in the ranger station on Walnut Creek. Sarah Day ministered to many of the rangers and early citizens. As the community grew, so too did its hospitals, including a Dr. Blanks's home, the Sonka home, and later the Plaza Hotel. In 2009, the hospital completed a $100 million expansion into the state-of-the-art Guadalupe Regional Medical Center, serving the surrounding counties. (Courtesy of Stanley Naumann.)

In 2009, Betty Ann Matthies was Seguin's mayor, the second woman to hold the position. Her enthusiasm has touched not only the city council, but also the community. She represents the spirit of Seguin in terms of controlled growth, appreciation of diversity, and the community working together. The spirit of Seguin's founders continues in today's municipal and county governments. (Courtesy of Betty Ann Matthies.)

It is only fitting to close with the statue of Juan Seguin in the city's inner block. The statue represents more than the man though. It is as if he is not only saluting the pioneers who named the town after him, but that he is also saluting and encouraging those who came after him to pursue the future with confidence, fearlessness, and integrity. (Courtesy of Stanley Naumann.)

Visit us at
arcadiapublishing.com